LET'S TALK LIFE

POETRY

BY

ABHILASHA BAFNA

INDIA • SINGAPORE • MALAYSIA

ISBN

Hardcase 979-8-89322-809-0
Paperback 979-8-89277-874-9

INDEX

FOREWORD

In the realm of literature, poetry stands as a timeless vessel through which we navigate the depths of human experience. It captures the essence of life in its purest form, distilling emotions, memories, and reflections into words that resonate with the soul. The pages of this book unfold like a tapestry, woven with threads of life's myriad moments - moments of joy, sorrow, love, and resilience.

"Let's Talk Life" invites us to embark on a journey of self-discovery and understanding. The author explores the complexities of existence via the lens of lyrical elegance. Each verse serves as a testament to the richness of human experience, inviting readers to explore the complexities of their own lives.

Life, with all its intricacies, is a mosaic of stories waiting to be told. In these pages, we encounter the echoes of laughter shared among friends, the sacrifice, the ache of loss that reverberates through the silence of solitude, the power of silence, the healing and the triumph of the human spirit in the face of adversity. Through evocative imagery and lyrical prose, the poet breathes life into these moments, inviting us to bear witness to the beauty and exquisiteness of our existence.

At its core, poetry is a conversation - a dialogue between the poet and the reader, between the past and the present, between the known and the unknown. It is a bridge that spans the chasm of human experience, connecting hearts and minds across time and space. In "Let's Talk Life," the author extends an invitation to engage in this dialogue to ponder, to reflect, and to find solace in the shared experience of being alive and to acknowledge the feelings which make us human.

As we journey through these pages, may we be reminded of the interconnectedness of our lives - the threads that bind us together, the stories that shape us, and the moments that define us. May we find comfort in the knowledge that, though our paths may diverge, we are united by the universal tapestry of human experience.

In a world where words often fail to capture the depth of our emotions, poetry stands as a beacon of hope, a beacon that illuminates the darkness, guiding us towards understanding, empathy, and connection. "Let's Talk Life" is a testament to the power of language to transcend barriers, to touch hearts, and to inspire change.

So let us embark on this journey together, dear reader. Let us immerse ourselves in the beauty of these verses, and let us discover, within the pages of this book, the true essence of what it means to be alive.

– Gargi Kulkarni

INTRODUCTION

Abhilasha Bafna is a poet and blogger from Mumbai. She is inspired by the Bhagavad Gita and the life experiences of herself and others. She writes about emotions, joy, sorrows, depression, setback, comeback, and the experiences of life. Her poems are direct from the core of her heart, exhibiting different life experiences and her love for psychology as well as understanding and analyzing the same. This is her first poetry book. You can find more of her work on her blog website [letstalklife.co] by Abhilasha Bafna and her Instagram blog with the same name.

HOW She STARTED AND WHAT'S THE PURPOSE?

Being an enthusiast reader and learner, she loved reading and learning new things and when she read Master of all: "BHAGAVAT GITA", from where she was enlightened deeply with the meaning and essence of her life more clearly making her take the initiative to write publicly rather than writing long paragraphs just for her closed ones to motivate and cheer them up on emotions, heartbreaks, depression and how life is and it could be. She started writing on Quora and her words were so powerful and motivating others, that made her create her own blog page with a bigger dream to help others rather than writing it just as a hobby.

As she started getting recognition on a very small front but sooner, she realized the essence of her words making her reflect on her truer self and starting her own blog website as well as Instagram blog.

The purpose of starting her own website is to talk as well as discuss and share the different opinions about life, its meaning, the practical approach that can be used to deal with the situations, depression, anxieties, or whatever fancy word one use's.

She has seen things through her life and experiences that made her realize that people don't let their heart out.

They don't discuss the actual problems or share their vulnerabilities and fear.

They don't discuss what's bothering them mentally and how that's affecting their life, career, relationships and so on.

And Author herself experiencing this drawback of not reaching out for help, she took the initiative to write on it and connect with people more and more through this, to make them see world as a safe place, where each and every human is allowed to be vulnerable at times, express it and heal through it.

Further, Author Answers to a general question, commonly asked : WHY PEOPLE DON'T REACH OUT?

Because there comes *fear of being judged, being called mental or weak, fear of being abandoned, status, reputation, fear of what people will say* and so much more.

People think, analyze, and calculate, the reasons for not letting their heart out, even if they are suffering because of this.

They suffocate within, trying to find the way, to figure out their life, finding answers, asking questions that-

Why them?

When will this get over?

How to overcome this?

But they'll never talk about it, because may be they are not been enlightened on how important one's mental health and it should be taken care of the same way one takes care of their own body physically, to be nourished from time to time.

In Gita Lord Krishna says in the Bhagavad Gita that the mind can be controlled by constant "practice and detachment." Lord says that wherever and whenever the mind wanders, due to its flickering and unsteady nature, we must bring it back under the control of the Self.

So, author here wants you to be carefree and let your heart out without the fear of being judged, feel your emotions, talk about it, connect with people and hear them out.

To read more the about the author and author's work, visit the given links as a QR Code below

WHO AM I?

I am the reader,
And my own cheerleader,
Leading my life as a leader.

I am the writer,
And the fighter

I am the observer
And the preserver.

I am the creature
Having different features,

I am the learner
And the earner.

I am the power,
Who is not a victim any longer.

AMBITION

I have an ambition,
That gives me the inspiration to stand out the
competition.

I have an ambition,
That makes me work without any condition.

I have an ambition,
That doesn't make any distraction a temptation,
Because my ambition is the only addiction.

I have an Ambition,
That makes me work without any conditions.

I have an ambition,
That always updates me with a newer edition.

I have an ambition,
That has given me the recognition.

WARRIOR

Hey Girl
How are you?

I know you have unsolved questions in your
mind,
But all your questions will be solved and soon
unwind.

You know why darling?
Because you are true from your heart that is
beautiful and kind.
I know it's difficult, it's difficult for you to
observe and let it go all as if you are blind.

But girl,
You are different,
You are different from everyone,
You are kind,
You are lovable sunshine,
You are strong and divine,
You are a warrior who is born to outshine.

Please don't resign,
Because a warrior makes it all align.

Please don't resign
Because soon everything will be fine.

LOVE

Hey love!
Happy to mention the selection,
That refurbished my complexion.

So good to have a connection,
That has no feeling of dejection.

Your affection gives me the direction,
With a newer perception.

You are the Interconnection,
That didn't need a protection.

All of my frustrations and fear of doubts,
Were made simpler by adding clarity and the
solution,
Bringing me back the confidence that I lost in all
this chaos long back.

Oh love!
You are the right selection,
That I would always love to mention.

HIM

You love him,
You want him,
You desire him,
You cherish him,
You forgive him,
You hold him.

You swim in his thoughts,
Goes dim with the effects of his blocks,
But you forgive again with a smile again,
You love again, empathize again,
You give again, yield again.

You are all of him,
But is he all of you?

UP'S & DOWN'S

Lately,
Life has become a see-saw!
One end goes up, the other goes down.

Same is with the life,
When finally, I make a progress,
Life has some other plans to depress.
I plan to move on,
Life brings the past amidst, to intrude on.

I say okay let's wrap, as it was all a scrap,
Life says, No! Let's Unwrap,
And recap the trap that led me to collapse.

The more I tried to leave the past behind and run,
Life makes me face it in front,
I know, running away is not the solution,
But sometimes running is better than the
dissolution.

So, let me run unless and until my true form
returns,
As it's better than the dissolution!

PATCH-UP

I danced,
As the phase of grief and anger just passed.
He asked for the forgiveness, one time last.
I glanced through his eyes to his heart,
Waiting to be romanced.

And, I danced,
As my heart romanced.
And this time,
It was a level advanced.

I said, why not take a chance,
So, I took a glance
And forgave him for the game of chance,
And, I danced,
As it was the love at first glance.

And I danced,
As he was once again here with the idea of
romance, and only romance,
So, yes, I danced.

Because it was us patching up again,
With the new chapter of romance.
So, yes, I danced, loving his every sight of glance,
Filled with love and romance.

SWEET GESTURES

He bought flowers,
On his way to home from work today.
He kissed my forehead,
With some donuts ahead.

He made me sit on his chair,
Feeding me the food I prepared,
Feeding me with his own hands
And his adorable glance that was stuck all over
me,
And this time, it was Not by chance.

It was the sweet gestures,
That made the years easier for us with some
adventures.

He picked me up from the market,
Assuring I was safe,
He lifted the bags,
Assuring I don't drain.

He cleared the air,
So that the vision is clear ahead,
Vanishing all the insecurities I had,
That once was the reason that I was scared.

It was the sweet gestures,
That made the years easier for us with some
adventures.

COLD PLAY

In the morning,
We had breakfast & left for the meetings,
And there were no morning greetings.

And the day passed,
Working and streaming,
And there were no greetings till the evening.

We were home in the evening,
All set at the dining for a dinner, with no good
evenings.
And the days passed Battling with the same
routine,
Where there was no communing,
And just the formal meetings.

The meetings were silent,
With a lot of screaming's echoing within,
Because it was the cold play hitting.
And our extra ordinary love,
Turned into not so casual but a strangers'
meetings.

A FRIEND

The one having no jealousy on the accomplishments
The one who is ready for you to take punishments
The one, who doesn't see you as a competition.

The one who is selfless,
The one who prays for you.

The one who changes,
But doesn't let your bond change,
The one who stays,
Even if you were away.

The one who needs no explanations
The one who listens to your heart without any
communications.

The one who respects the relation,
And your emotions,
The one who values your time and affection.

The one who is the motivation,
When you are down with frustrations.

The one who requires no invitation,
And the one who have no stop at Ego Station.

YOU CREATED A MESS

I cried writing those paragraphs
But you read them just as a text
I died reading those lines
But you denied reading the emotions

No no, I was not a mess
It was just a game of chess

You played,
I defended,
You won,
I lost.

You are the king today,
But not having a queen you love till day,
Because you played like a chess,
That created a mess!

IT'S JUST A FATE

It's not a story
It's not a play
It's not a script either
It's a Reality,
That just checked.

Yeah, even I expected a different version as you did,
But you see, things are not always as expected
and straight.

It's not the end,
But that's not how things were to be meant.

But I am still great for the life lessons learned that
we hate.
No, I am not upset as I considered this as my Fate,
That left us to debate.
It's just a fate that showed us the way Straight!

HOW ARE YOU?

Hey,
It's me again...

How are you?
I hope you are not getting the wrong clue.

Clue about me asking you again about you,
It is just a concern that made me Brew.
Yeah, it was a concern than too,

Coming up with no explanations for your
misunderstandings
For than as well as now too.

I just owe you to ask about your well-being,
For letting me learn the best lessons of my life,
Making me stronger,
When you left behind.

So yeah, I do owe you, and do tell me,
How are you?

GRACEFUL

Hey Angel
Is your life beautiful,
Or your fighting charm making it more graceful?
Though it's painful,
But how you still stay, so faithful?
Your energy is blissful
That makes the environment colourful.

Hey Angel,
You are a queen,
Who inspires the castle with her grace,
Who is wonderful with her pace,
Even when the things around are ungrateful.

Hey Angel
You are a queen,
Who is emotional and dreadful,
And powerful,
A queen working hard to conquer her dream,

Though dreadful!
Your hard work is appreciable,
And the journey of yours has made it more
beautiful,

Hey Angel,
How you are so graceful?

CONFIDENT

It was a rainy day,
With clouds all around
Making the vision smoggiest, round the ground,
With the sound of dazzling storm in the town.

And a voice interrupted the dazzling sound of the
storm uptown,
"Will you be able to do it? Are you aware of your
capabilities to be on a fairground?

And suddenly,
The sound of the storm was down,
My mind was repeating the question of doubt in
the background:
"Will you be able to do it?"
"Are you aware of your capabilities?"

That made me think once again!
Yes, that made me think again!
But this time I was not questioning my own
capabilities but the people around,
Who always took me down.

But this time I was ready for a showdown,
And not the breakdown,
And I begin to cut off people who were not so
profound.

And my confidence,
Once again let me rebound.

SACRIFICE – THE MOTHER

From not having the last piece of meal,
To not buying the things she like.

From spending the quality time with her kids,
To not attending the kitties anymore.

From not having a dream of her own,
To giving up her desires and dreams for the
dreams of your own.

From not wearing new clothes on Diwali
To getting you your favourite dress that you
asked for.

From not having the money for herself,
To fulfill your needs from the bunch of savings of
her own.

From being a little girl with dreams in her eyes,
To being a mother living for your dreams now
and then,
As if it's the dream of her own.

From being a little girl,
To a mother, carving the path of sacrifices,
Is this the only thing she owns?

JEALOUSY

I don't know,
What they ever wanted,
Either, they were threatened,
Or were they protective,
Or were they just fearful, of losing their position.

Nothing ever justified me their behaviour
It made me feel their high insecurities,
Them wanting all that I had in my life vanity,
All the attributes and possessions,
That were hard earned with some flaws &
perfections.

Never they seem to show some appreciation,
All they ever shown me was my imperfections,
And the rejections,
Some Questioning my profession,
That more sounded like their failures &
depression,
And the jealousy, that have no solution.

I don't know what they ever wanted,
But they seem to be in possession,
Of their failures and depression,
That made them jealous of my progression.

INFATUATION

When we met,
It was the month of monsoon,
And You were just a stranger,
With us having a formal relation.

Your passion and energy,
Became so captivating,
That made you such a fascination.

Though you were just a stranger,
I was head over heels in your imagination,
That made me sleepless and passionate,
To have you, was my obsession.

Your flawless features,
Made me think of you 24/7,
You being always in my head,
Made me think this was the love that I have
always craved for, to get in.

But sooner it started diminishing,
When I couldn't accept you as a whole,
When I couldn't accept you as you with your
flaws,
That made me realise,
It was just an Infatuation,
That took up my mind.

DEPRESSION

It was a good time,
Unless, you made me lose interest in the activities
I loved,
Unless, you interfered in my routines and made it
all about you,
Unless you made me feel sad all day long
constantly,
Living me with no energy and low in mood, that
made me vulnerable in and out.

It was a good time,
Unless, you made me beg for your attention,
Unless you made me lose my self-confidence,
Unless you had an affair out of this relationship
with a clear intention,
Unless you call me out with names when I made
confrontation.

It was a good time,
Unless you gave me a ton of Depression!

POWER

She was authoritative,
She was a leader,
She had the energy,
That influenced people within seconds as she
was a keeper.

She was a queen,
With her own kingdom and a throne,
She was respected,
And loved.

She was a change,
And a justice queen,
Who never let the wrongdoers go clean.

She was a lady,
Who had the power to rule like a queen.

COMEBACK

She was hurt,
She was beaten,
She was injured by her closed ones.

Her voice was sealed,
And they made her sit with doors closed
unrevealed.

But She was a lioness,
And was at a war inside,
That made her break all the doors,
Making a comeback in the world of her own
With a Roar.

BOUNDLESS

A lady with the fire,
Having the limitless desires,
And the power to acquire,
That made others feel inspired.

Wearing an attire,
That all admired.

Having the dreams higher,
With the energy to achieve it all like a fighter,
And create a future colourful and brighter.

She was a lady,
Limitless,
Who had no boundaries,
To achieve her desires,
She was boundless,
Having profound love in herself!

EMOTIONS

Emotions, a very short-lived feeling
That comes from a Cause, known to us

Emotions, let us communicate with others,
Emotions, can be expressed,
And can be controlled as well

Emotions let us understand other people
As well as, it let others understand us,

Emotions originates from our thoughts
Thoughts that give us the feeling of sadness or
anger,
Feeling of being Happy or surprised,
Feeling of being scared out of fear or disgusted
Feeling of joy or trust,
Feeling of affection or love,
All these feelings are born,
Depending on how we think and what we think
on our own.

Emotions are basic,
That reflects our behaviour and sensations

Emotions are lively,
That reflects our relationships,
And the life it adds to it.

Emotions are short-lived,
But its effect on others can be long term and
forever sometimes.

Emotions are basic,
That must be expressed aesthetic.

Emotions are basic,
That must be expressed not just with a logic,
But with a feeling,
That doesn't hurt others,
But also, it must not be hidden within,
Because that Will be a cheating as well as
suffocating,
With oneself and the others trusting.
So, it must be expressed and handled with a
pinch of care as well as logic,
Because though it may be short lived,
But it may have an effect long term and forever,
As it's a feeling that is short-lived, but can have
an effect long-lived.

OH LIFE!

Oh life!
Why are you treating me like this,
Why are you alienating me with yourself through
all the conflicts.

The moment I take a step to move forward,
You pull me back.

The moment I start living,
You make me wish to die.

The moment I smile,
You make me cry.

Oh life!
Tell me, why are you treating me like this,
Why are you alienating me with yourself through
all the conflicts.

HE WAS TOXIC

He was toxic,
So, I decided to leave him,
And the day I left him,
He said I was being unreasonable and selfish
making him feel used and sick!

And stunned me replied:

What about the times you left me,
What about the times you made me cry all the
while, then let it be day or a whole night,
What about the times you gave me anxieties and
the depression,
What about the times you played me,
What about the times you used me financially,
What about the times you disrespected me,
What about the times you insulted me for your
so-called cheap love, another infatuation,
What about the times you harmed me mentally
every single moment,

What about the times you being selfish, who left
me in the times of my down moments of life...
What about the times when you continued your
double standards every single day...
What about the times you used me?

And he replied,

You are being unreasonable and selfish making
him feel used and sick!

So, to prove him right, I became unreasonable
and selfish at once,
And guess what...
There was finally an end to this relationship and
an end to my innocence, that led me here.

FALLING APART

Everything was falling,
And all other things were drifting and departing,
Away From me and within me.

I tried longer and longer to hold on,
To be patient,
And away from a mental depression.
To be strong,
And face the setbacks with no regrets and being
upset.

I tried longer and longer to hold on,
But now I am drowning and struggling,
To get up,
To face the fears,
To face the break downs given by my loved ones,
To please others to stay,
To get back my confidence,
To get up and go to work the very next day,

To be hopeful, that the situations and people will
be improved someday,
Bringing me back from the black hole that I am
staying in, currently with no coming back.

Yes, I tried longer and longer to hold on,
But now I am falling apart and it's time now to
move on.

INSECURITY

Insecurity is loud
That sounds loud, though not spoken aloud!

Insecure is the one,
Who questions rather than appreciating others.

Insecure is the one,
Who ignores the achievements of others.

Insecure is the one,
Who is jealous of others succeeding and making
progress.

Insecure is the one,
Who plays the role of toxic;
Be it a friend, relative or peers in one's life.

Insecure is the one,
Who loves seeing you down.

Insecurity is loud
That sounds loud, though not spoken aloud!

ILLUSION

He was the role model and the inspiration,
He moved me by his passion
He was the man of his words,
And a family man,
Having a beautiful wife and a daughter, who was
his pride.
Depicting all the qualities that a gentleman
should have.
He was a fighter and the Godfather
He was the man whom I worshipped than no
other!

He was a man,
That made me believe that everything about him
was so perfect.

Unless...
Unless I found,
Unless I found that the image he created and
portrayed all these years,
The image that I believed in blindly,

The image that made me worship him,
The image...
Was unreal and illusionary.

And that my trust in him was broken when,
I caught him having an extra marital affair with
not one but more than one of "my classmates"
I caught him having an affair with my classmates,
That was denied every time I confronted.

That was denied every time I confronted
But it surely cleared all my doubts,
All my confusions,
All the fog that was formed about his picture-
perfect image,
Was Unreal and a mere Illusion.

And he was the man,
Whom once I called professor and my
motivation,
But came out to be a mere illusion.

HE WAS TOO LATE!

He called and accepted,
That he was wrong,
And was used by the girl for whom he made me
feel like a crap all this long,
He wept and screamed,
That I was right.

He elaborated again,
The efforts I use to take,
And the genuine characteristic I always
portrayed,
And how he misses the presence of me,
That use to make him so well-settled and aware,

He was a senior,
And my friend,
Who was too late,
To realize his mistakes.

However,
All the time over the call,
When he wept and accepted his mistakes,

I was thinking what made him call me now, so late,
Was this his another game?
That took him so long to plan it all over again?
And I was thinking,
What made him took so long
To realize his own mistakes,
Because now I was well aware about his
intentions
That would never trap me in again.

AND I WAS RIGHT

He cried,
And admitted I was right.

He cried,
And admitted his mistakes uptight.

He cried,
Hoping once again to play a game that makes me
feel,
That he is right.

He cried,
But he indirectly denied.

He cried,
But elsewhere he repeated, for what he actually
cried.

And he cried,
That once again confirmed me his intentions,
That were not right.

And I was Right,
For knowing him, who was never right,
And an unchanged person with no pride.

And I was right!

SHE MADE A MISTAKE!

She is not clean,
She has made mistakes too,
And the bad ones, the real bad ones.
She made a mistake,
By prioritizing others than herself,
By letting them use her.

She made a mistake,
Because she always believed in generosity,
Because she always wanted to spread love,
Because she always wanted to heal others,
Because she always was a giver, giving it all
to others though she was not having it all in
abundance.

Yes, she made a mistake,
For forgiving others again and again for their
misdoings.
For accepting a disrespect, as she misunderstood
it as love and frustration of them.

Yes, she made a mistake,
For choosing a wrong person always,
Though she always had the right one.

Yes, she made a mistake,
For contributing her time and energy on the non-
deserving,
And ignoring the ones who truly deserved.

Yes, she made a huge-huge mistake,
For forgetting herself,
For the sake of others.

REALITY CHECK AND
THE BROKEN GIRL

No sooner, but later,
Life gave her a reality check,
Showing the masked faces unmasked,
And telling me, "Girl, Step away."

But, as usual
She was a girl,
And being a girl,
You know she never steps away,
But instead tries to fix it.

A girl tries to fix everything,
That is broken, then be it a furniture or a man.

A girl tries to fix everything,
That is broken, then be it a furniture or a man,
Though that may leave her heart broken there
and then.

And the life gave her again,
Some reality checks,

And this time it showed her,
The cruel and selfish species of human they were,
Whom she was trying to fix,
But as they were among these cruel ones,
They never appreciated her efforts, and her
genuineness,
And the kind heart,
That she was here to fix them from unbroken to a
whole again,
But life had other plans,
And gave her the reality check,
Showing the masked faces, unmasked.

And this time she was broken,
This time she was broken hard,
Gathering the scattered pieces of her all around,
Gathering everything that was fallen apart in a
count.

This time it was her,
Who was broken,
And was in the need of fixation,

Yes, this time she was in the need of fixation,
Who was left formless and aimless,
By the species of a human kind,
Who were among the cruel and selfish minds,
Whose masked faces were unmasked,
Giving the girl a reality check.
That made her feel worthless,
But she will surely, make a comeback.

THE POWER OF SILENCE

The day,
I started ignoring,

The day,
I stopped responding

The day
I started more and more listening

The day,
I stopped answering back the morons
Though they provoked me to the hell in gallons,
Though they blamed me for the things I
shouldn't be,
Though they tried to prove themselves superior
and correct, even when they were not,
Though they tried to justify themselves on their
wrong deeds,
Though they tried to pull me down,
Though they played their games all the way
around,

Was the day,
I became mightier.

Was the day,
I was grown mentally strong.

Was the day,
I respected myself more.

Was the day,
I learned dealing with morons.

Was the day,
I learned that silence have given me more power
than any other in this universe,
And I learned the power of silence.

SELF-HELP

I was broken,
Left with no emotions.

I was tortured,
Left with the trace of traumas to be nurtured.

I was lifeless,
That made me even more careless.

I was frowning,
That led me drowning.

I was disowned,
When all I needed was to be owned.

I was exhausted
Who was tired surviving.

I was blamed to be lazy and unmotivated
Recommended and lectured with the directions
and the values I lacked,
But all I was in the need of was a self-help.

HEALING

She wore no more scars,
Fighting all her fears like a star.

She started going to places,
Meeting new people, connecting with them,
That once she avoided out of fear and her past
traces.

She was confident now to stand out in public,
And stand up for herself,
That once she didn't due to the scars invisible,
that led her to death.

She was reborn again,
Because this time she was healing,
With the traumas she was given again and again.

Healing with the depression,
That made her quit, her profession.

She was reborn again,
Because this time she was healing,

With the battle going on within her,
That made her drain through all this pain
That stuck on her like a stain,
Making her indecisive with no brain.

She was born again,
Because this time she was healing,
With all those pains,
That she will never let come to her again,
And she was borne again,
As she healed herself from all the pain.

A GIRL WITH NO REGRETS

Hey life!
It's been a while, we haven't met,
Seems like you are quite upset.

Okay, give me a chance to reset,
So that there will be no regrets.

And the Regrets will never offset,
So, let's make a bet, to clear all the debts.

I may take time to set,
I may also fail to reset,
But I'll be satisfied for the efforts I made to make
it all correct,
Making you never forget the girl with no regrets...

GOOD MORNING

It was a pleasant day,
Birds chirping,
People chanting,
And some on the morning walks
Having beautiful talks.
And The Sun rose in the east,
With its beaming light on all beyond leaving no
one beneath.

And on the table of the breakfast,
Me and my brother fighting,
For the slice of toast
Made by our mom for both.
Heading towards work
With a new day and a new start,
Because after every dark night,
The Sun rises from the east,
With its beaming light on all beyond leaving no
one beneath.
Wishing you all a bright day,
And a very Good-Morning.

BLAME-GAME

Some blamed their parents,
Some blamed their friends,
Some blamed their luck,
Some blamed their destinies,
Some blamed universe,
Some blamed the creator,
Some blamed the destroyer,
Some blamed the karmic actions,
And some blamed the evils.

No one blamed themselves,
You know why?
Blaming others was easiest to all, by all and for
all.

And some blamed.........
Because it was the easiest way out,
To let go of pain and the mistakes of their own,
That let them down and lead them down forever.

It was all the game of a mindset,
That lead them to play a blame game.

An so they blamed,
Because it was the easiest way out.

LONELINESS

I have a family,
And the friends,
I have colleagues,
And the workplace.

I loved everyone,
And everyone too loved me,
I worked harder for everyone,
And was praised a-much little but that was okay
for me, because at least they praised me, though
a little.

I was always surrounded by people,
But still couldn't escape my loneliness,
That made me hollow inside,

But yet there was I, smiling and working for the
people for whom I shall even die!

MY LIFE IS A STORY

My life is a story,
A full budget,
And an award-winning story.

It is an action based,
And also, with the peace.
It is filled with conflicting issues,
And off course a ton of comedy that made me live
at ease.
It calls out some cheaters,
And also, the lovers.
It is also a love story,
Having a crazy Romeo,
Who makes my life beautiful and a masterpiece.
It calls out some haters,
And also, the well-wishers.

It has me,
A fighter,
And the writer,
Who believes in writing her own destiny with her
god to the greater.

A creator of all up comings in her life,
And the destroyer of all things out of life.
A lover,
And the giver,
A loser,
As well as a winner.

It has me,
Who is a great fighter.

My life is a story,
That has me with a distinct and the most
important character.

My life is a story,
That deserves an award, to outstand as its special
character.

NATURE

I admire being in nature,
It's calm and peaceful,
It's pleasant and blissful,
It's charismatic and energetic,
It's the answer to all the queries,
It's the relaxation to all the worries,
It's tempting and motivating,
It's cool as well as warm,
It's hard as well as soft,
It's the universe made by our great lords.

GREAT-GREAT DAD

The one who cares,
The one who loves,
The one who protects,
The one who guides,
The one who yells when wrong,
The one who slaps on the mistakes,
The one who caresses even being far away,
The one who never expresses you the love that's within,
Who is strict outside but is soft by the soul within ,
Is the **Great-Great Dad** that makes you capable to stand alone.

WHY?

I asked,
Why always I need to sacrifice?
Because you have given a way more than required.

Why I am always neglected?
Because you dumped yourself for them.

Why my efforts are never counted?
Because you made them for the wrong ones.

Why this is happening to me?
Because you yourself let it happen again and
again.

Why they left me shattered?
Because you gave them control.

Why I am getting back this for all the good I did?
Because you were too good to the bad ones indeed.

Why I am not getting what I truly deserve?
Because you have neglected what you already
have.

Why it has to be this way?
Because that's the way you have chosen.

Why me?
Because your choices and fate chosen you to this.

CRISIS

We were into crisis
That broke us into pieces
But we were firm,
Holding them together with stiffness.

We worked
Day and night to make it all right
We loved and care
To be each other's strength
We fought
Taking out all the frustrations that led us to
drought

We drowned
We frowned
But not much,
As we knew how to rebound.

Our love was the strength,
And caring a support,
That closed all the way for the crisis,
To let us deport.

Yes, we were into crisis,
That taught us the meaning of life,
To write a thesis with our own entitles!

BREAKING THE GOLDEN CAGE

Life was hard and dark,
When no one allowed me to be my truer self,
On the journey,
That I so wanted to embark.

I waited,
For them to trust me and let me begin,
But they were into the abode of caging me in the
golden cage, again and again.
That made my identity go futile,
Making me feel worthless,
Though I had so much to achieve.

So, I decided,
To begin the journey,
That I had dreamt,
Though it may cost me losing them all, boarding
on it.
Because it was the journey of my dreams,
That would never snatch away my identity from me,
Like they did.

So, I decided,
To begin the journey,
That I had dreamt,
By breaking the golden cage,
That set me beneath.

SOLO

I loved people around,
But I liked more to be solo.

They were good, too good,
But I liked more to be solo.

Solo movies,
Solo lunches,
Solo dinners,
Solo trips,
Solo mourning,
Solo sulking,
Solo loving,
Solo learning,
Because I liked it more to be solo.

Yes, I liked it more to be solo
As it made me know myself better,
As it made me learn from the mistakes,
As it gives me the best solutions to all the
problems,
As it answers to all the questions that I look after,

As it makes me meet an expert of all, none other than myself,
That makes me more sharp tackling it all on my own to be the best.

Because I love being more solo.

SELF-LOVE AND APPRECIATION

Sitting at a river bank,
Thinking what was the chance,
That I would again romance,
Even after getting hurt still with his
remembrance.

Sitting at a river bank,
I thought,
Why I gave him so many chances,
When I was getting no remittance?

Sitting at a river bank,
I thought,
What made him leave me with so reluctance,
When all I did was, a pure romance.

Sitting at a river bank,
Thinking of why I got no appreciation and love,
For the efforts I made,

For the sacrifices I made,
For the beauty I have within,
Reflecting outside with a beam.

And while thinking,
I observed the beauty of the nature
Who never gets an appreciation
But still stands affirm and charming,
Loving its truer form and self, with no
expectations.
And that is where the beauty lies,
In the self-love and appreciation,
That answered my all the above questions.

MAN, MADE IN HEAVEN

So,
I was all-ready,
After a breakdown,
To see someone who would love me in my ups
and downs.

He was a man with the beliefs,
And principles,
That made him wiser and charming,
Holding his own essence.

He was a man,
Who was loyal and pure,
That made me trust the essence of love again.

He was the man of his words,
That made me believe in the promises we made.

He was a man with pride,
Who did all the rights,
And was sorry when wrong by his side,
That assured me, I am safe on this ride.

He was a man
"Made in heaven"
That healed me within, leaving no piece of
grievance.

He was a man,
"Made in Heaven."
That made me trust the essence of love again.

SUPPORT

I started,
Where I was left,
And I drowned again,
Because I was left at the edge

But there was a hand of support,
That made me stand even on the edge.

A support that made me alive again,
Without any quest.

A support that filled me with the confidence,
That was drowned from the point of edge.

And I was left,
Where, he forwarded his hand in the support,
That made me alive again.

FINALLY, I WAS HEALING

I left the places,
That made me drown and frown,
I left the people,
That took me a way-way down,
I left the places,
That used me just for their benefits,
I left the people,
With no principal's and morals,
Who still got horses to talk about me,
Just to save them on all their wrongdoings.

I left,
The one who were the criminals,
For harming me and many others,
Incurred me the losses,
That could never be recovered,
That left me with a huge mental breakdown.

I left,
Without revealing his truth to the world,
Though they made me look like a criminal,

Just because they were insecure as well as scared
enough,
To face me and the truth, that if revealed will take
him down.

I left,
The one who was not worth it to hold on,
And started recovering from the mental traumas
And the depression that I carried so long.
And finally, I was healing,
From all those mental breakdowns.

LIFE

Life is tough,
And sometimes rough,
It makes us weep,
And also let it all sweep,
It has levels, that when cleared,
Takes us to the next, the advanced one being
triggered.
Easy at first,
That gets tough with the each passing level with
a thrust,
And if failed, we need to give a re-attempt,
And keep giving,
Unless and until we clear it and pass, to move on
to the next one.

It teaches us the lessons,
That makes us wiser and experienced,
It's like a seed growing into a tree,
A tree if watered and maintained well,
It will bear the fruits that taste's the best.

It's definitely tough at times,
That gets easier with the hard-work and time.
Don't abandon, just get it done,
To be on the path of life to walk and run.

Abhilasha Bafna   91

NOTES